# CHRISTMAS SONGS
## FOR CLASSICAL PLAYERS

ISBN 978-1-4950-9880-2

To access companion recorded piano accompaniments online, visit:
**www.halleonard.com/mylibrary**

Enter Code
2674-7412-1946-7622

**HAL•LEONARD®**
7777 W. BLUEMOUND RD. P.O. BOX 13819 MILWAUKEE, WI 53213

Visit Hal Leonard Online at
**www.halleonard.com**

Pianists on the recordings: [1] Brendan Fox, [2] Richard Walters

The price of this publication includes access to companion recorded piano accompaniments online,
for download or for streaming, using the unique code found on the title page.
Visit **www.halleonard.com/mylibrary** and enter the access code.

# The Christmas Song
## (Chestnuts Roasting on an Open Fire)

Music and Lyric by Mel Tormé
and Robert Wells
Arranged by Richard Walters

# Christmas Time Is Here
from A CHARLIE BROWN CHRISTMAS

Words by Lee Mendelson
Music by Vince Guaraldi
Arranged by Joshua Parman

# The Christmas Waltz

Words by Sammy Cahn
Music by Jule Styne
Arranged by Hank Powell

**Moderate Waltz**

# Have Yourself a Merry Little Christmas
### from MEET ME IN ST. LOUIS

Words and Music by Hugh Martin
and Ralph Blane
Arranged by Celeste Avery

# The Most Wonderful Time of the Year

Words and Music by Eddie Pola
and George Wyle
Arranged by Luke Duane

# I Wonder As I Wander
## (Appalachian Carol)

By John Jacob Niles
Adapted and arranged by Celeste Avery

# CHRISTMAS SONGS
## FOR CLASSICAL PLAYERS

ISBN 978-1-4950-9880-2

Flute

# The Christmas Song
## (Chestnuts Roasting on an Open Fire)

Music and Lyric by Mel Tormé
and Robert Wells
Arranged by Richard Walters

**Rather slowly, steadily**

# Christmas Time Is Here

from A CHARLIE BROWN CHRISTMAS

Words by Lee Mendelson
Music by Vince Guaraldi
Arranged by Joshua Parman

# The Christmas Waltz

Words by Sammy Cahn
Music by Jule Styne
Arranged by Hank Powell

# Have Yourself a Merry Little Christmas

from MEET ME IN ST. LOUIS

Words and Music by Hugh Martin
and Ralph Blane
Arranged by Celeste Avery

# I Wonder As I Wander
### (Appalachian Carol)

By John Jacob Niles
Adapted and arranged by Celeste Avery

# The Most Wonderful Time of the Year

Words and Music by Eddie Pola
and George Wyle
Arranged by Luke Duane

12

Flute

# I'll Be Home for Christmas

Words and Music by Kim Gannon
and Walter Kent
Arranged by Brendan Fox

# O Christmas Tree
### (O Tannenbaum)

16th century Silesian folksong
Arranged by Richard Walters

Flute

# Silver Bells
from the Paramount Picture THE LEMON DROP KID

Words and Music by Jay Livingston
and Ray Evans
Arranged by Luke Duane

# Sleigh Ride

Music by Leroy Anderson
Arranged by Celeste Avery

# Waltz of the Flowers
from *The Nutcracker*

Pyotr Il'yich Tchaikovsky
Arranged by Joshua Parman

**Tempo di Valse**

# White Christmas

from the Motion Picture Irving Berlin's HOLIDAY INN

Words and Music by
Irving Berlin
Arranged by Richard Walters

# I'll Be Home for Christmas

Words and Music by Kim Gannon
and Walter Kent
Arranged by Brendan Fox

**Moderately slow**

# O Christmas Tree
## (O Tannenbaum)

16th century Silesian folksong
Arranged by Richard Walters

# Sleigh Ride

Music by Leroy Anderson
Arranged by Celeste Avery

To Coda

**D.S. al Coda**

# Silver Bells
from the Paramount Picture THE LEMON DROP KID

Words and Music by Jay Livingston
and Ray Evans
Arranged by Luke Duane

# White Christmas
from the Motion Picture Irving Berlin's HOLIDAY INN

Words and Music by
Irving Berlin
Arranged by Richard Walters

# Waltz of the Flowers
from *The Nutcracker*

Pyotr Il'yich Tchaikovsky
Arranged by Joshua Parman

**Tempo di Valse**